EASY **INSTRUMENTAL PLAY-ALONG**

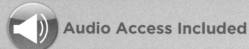
Audio Access Included

Visit **www.halleonard.com/mylibrary**

Enter Code

2510-9101-0591-5559

CLASSIC ROCK
FOR FLUTE

Audio Arrangements by Peter Deneff
Tracking, mixing, and mastering by BeatHouse Music

ISBN 978-1-4803-5446-3

7777 W. BLUEMOUND RD. P.O. BOX 13819 MILWAUKEE, WI 53213

For all works contained herein:
Unauthorized copying, arranging, adapting, recording, Internet posting, public performance,
or other distribution of the printed or recorded music in this publication is an infringement of copyright.
Infringers are liable under the law.

Visit Hal Leonard Online at
www.halleonard.com

CONTENTS

ANOTHER ONE BITES THE DUST

© 1980 QUEEN MUSIC LTD.
All Rights for the U.S. and Canada Controlled and Administered by BEECHWOOD MUSIC CORP.
All Rights for the world excluding the U.S. and Canada
 Controlled and Administered by EMI MUSIC PUBLISHING LTD.
All Rights Reserved   International Copyright Secured   Used by Permission

Words and Music by
JOHN DEACON

BORN TO BE WILD

Copyright © 1968 UNIVERSAL MUSIC PUBLISHING, A Division of UNIVERSAL MUSIC CANADA, INC.
Copyright Renewed
All Rights in the United States Controlled and Administered by UNIVERSAL MUSIC CORP.
All Rights Reserved   Used by Permission

Words and Music by
MARS BONFIRE

Moderate Rock

BROWN EYED GIRL

Copyright © 1967 UNIVERSAL MUSIC PUBLISHING INTERNATIONAL LTD.
Copyright Renewed
All Rights for the U.S. and Canada Controlled and Administered by
 UNIVERSAL - SONGS OF POLYGRAM INTERNATIONAL, INC.
All Rights Reserved   Used by Permission

Words and Music by
VAN MORRISON

EVERY BREATH YOU TAKE

© 1983 G.M. SUMNER
Administered by EMI MUSIC PUBLISHING LIMITED
All Rights Reserved   International Copyright Secured   Used by Permission

Words and Music by
STING

DUST IN THE WIND

© 1977 (Renewed 2005), 1978 EMI BLACKWOOD MUSIC INC. and DON KIRSHNER MUSIC
All Rights Controlled and Administered by EMI BLACKWOOD MUSIC INC.
All Rights Reserved   International Copyright Secured   Used by Permission

Words and Music by
KERRY LIVGREN

FLY LIKE AN EAGLE

Copyright © 1976 by Sailor Music
Copyright Renewed
All Rights Reserved   Used by Permission

Words and Music by
STEVE MILLER

UP AROUND THE BEND

Copyright © 1970 Jondora Music
Copyright Renewed
International Copyright Secured   All Rights Reserved

Words and Music by
JOHN FOGERTY

I HEARD IT THROUGH THE GRAPEVINE

© 1966 (Renewed 1994) JOBETE MUSIC CO., INC.
All Rights Controlled and Administered by EMI BLACKWOOD MUSIC INC.
 on behalf of STONE AGATE MUSIC (A Division of JOBETE MUSIC CO., INC.)
All Rights Reserved   International Copyright Secured   Used by Permission

Words and Music by NORMAN J. WHITFIELD
amd BARRETT STRONG

I SHOT THE SHERIFF

Copyright © 1974 Fifty-Six Hope Road Music Ltd. and Odnil Music Ltd.
Copyright Renewed
All Rights in North America Administered by Blue Mountain Music Ltd./Irish Town Songs (ASCAP)
  and throughout the rest of the world by Blue Mountain Music Ltd. (PRS)
All Rights Reserved

Words and Music by
BOB MARLEY

Moderately

OYE COMO VA

© 1963, 1970 (Renewed 1991, 1998) EMI FULL KEEL MUSIC
All Rights Reserved   International Copyright Secured   Used by Permission

Words and Music by
TITO PUENTE